# Shadows and Mirrors

## Unveiling the Psychology of Prejudice and Discrimination

**Freudian Trips**

# Copyright Page

# Disclaimer

The views and opinions expressed in this book are those of the author(s) and do not necessarily reflect the official policy or position of any other agency, organization, employer, or company. The contents of this book are for informational and educational purposes only and are not intended to serve as professional advice, diagnosis, or treatment.

The information provided in this book is believed to be accurate and reliable as of the date of publication. However, it may include some errors or inaccuracies, and no warranty or guarantee is provided regarding the accuracy, timeliness, or applicability of the content.

Readers are encouraged to consult with professional philosophers, educators, or other qualified professionals where appropriate for personalized advice. The author(s) and publisher shall not be liable for any loss, damage, or harm caused or alleged to be caused, directly or indirectly, by the information or ideas contained, suggested, or referenced in this book.

# Introduction: The Veiled Mind

## Defining Prejudice and Discrimination

Imagine walking through a dense fog where your vision is clouded, and you can only see shapes and shadows. This fog is like the unseen biases and prejudices that cloud our judgments and interactions with others. Understanding these hidden elements within us is like clearing the fog to see the world more clearly.

## Prejudice: The Unseen Bias

Prejudice is like having a pre-written script in our minds about certain groups of people. It's an unjustified, often negative, attitude towards an individual based solely on their membership in a specific group. Think of it as a mental shortcut, where our brain makes quick judgments based on limited information. For example, deciding someone is untrustworthy because they belong to a certain community, even though we know nothing else about them.

## Discrimination: Actions Born from Prejudice

If prejudice is the script, discrimination is the act. It's when we treat people differently and often unfairly, based on their group identity. This could range from not hiring someone because of their race, to crossing the street to avoid someone because of how they dress. Discrimination is the tangible, often painful result of prejudice.

## The Importance of Understanding Psychological Underpinnings

### The Iceberg of Our Minds

Our minds are like icebergs. What we see and acknowledge - our conscious thoughts and actions - is just the tip of the iceberg. Below the surface lies a vast world of unconscious biases and prejudices, unseen but powerful. These hidden biases influence how we view and treat others, often without us even realizing it.

### Why Understanding This Matters

**Self-Awareness:** We all have biases. Recognizing and understanding them is the first step in overcoming them. It's like turning on a light in a dark room - suddenly, we can see what was always there.

**Better Relationships:** Understanding our prejudices helps us build stronger, more authentic relationships. It allows us to connect with others based on who they truly are, rather than the labels we've unconsciously attached to them.

**A Fairer Society:** By understanding and addressing our biases, we contribute to a more just society. When we stop acting on our unfounded prejudices, we reduce discrimination, making our communities more inclusive and harmonious.

**Personal Growth:** Confronting our biases can be uncomfortable, but it's a crucial part of personal growth. It's like climbing a mountain - challenging, but the view from the top is worth it.

As we embark on this journey through the world of prejudice and discrimination, remember, this is about exploring the unseen parts of ourselves. It's not about blame or shame. It's about understanding the veiled mind and, through that understanding, creating a clearer, more compassionate view of the world and the people in it.

# Chapter 1: Historical Perspectives

**Evolutionary Basis of In-group vs. Out-group Dynamics**

**The Roots of Us vs. Them**

Long ago, when humans lived in small groups, survival depended on strong bonds among group members. These early humans needed to quickly distinguish between friends (in-group) and potential threats (out-group). This instinct, like an ancient security system, helped them survive in a world full of dangers.

**The In-group: A Circle of Trust**

The in-group, which consisted of family and close allies, was a circle of trust and cooperation. Within this circle, resources were shared, and there was mutual protection. The stronger this inner circle, the higher the chances of survival. Think of it as being on a team where everyone looks out for each other.

## The Out-group: The Unknown Others

On the flip side, those outside this circle – the out-group – were often seen as potential threats. Strangers might compete for resources or pose dangers. This suspicion towards outsiders was a defense mechanism. It's like being cautious around someone you've never met before.

## Societal Constructs and Historical Prejudices

### Building Walls Through History

As societies grew, the simple division of us vs. them became more complex. Groups started defining themselves not just by family ties but by language, religion, race, and territory. These categories formed invisible walls, creating divisions that went beyond physical survival.

### The Role of Power and Control

Throughout history, certain groups have used the idea of 'us vs. them' to gain or maintain power. By positioning their own group as superior or more deserving, they justified controlling resources and oppressing other groups. This has been a pattern in many societies, leading to deep-rooted prejudices and discrimination.

### Historical Prejudices: A Legacy

The prejudices we see today didn't just appear out of nowhere; they have deep historical roots. For example, colonialism spread the notion of racial superiority and inferiority across the world. These ideas, like bad seeds, were planted and grew over time, influencing societies' views on race and ethnicity.

### Society's Mirror: Reflecting and Reinforcing Prejudices

Societal norms and institutions often reflect and reinforce historical prejudices. Laws, educational content, media portrayals, and even everyday language can perpetuate outdated and unjust ideas about certain groups. It's like a mirror that keeps showing an old, distorted image, even though the reality has changed.

Understanding the historical context of in-group vs. out-group dynamics, and how societies have constructed and perpetuated prejudices, helps us see that these are not natural or unchangeable truths. They are like old stories passed down through generations. Recognizing them as such allows us to start writing new narratives, ones that are inclusive and based on mutual respect and understanding. In this chapter, we've journeyed through time to understand the roots of 'us vs. them' and how this primitive instinct morphed into the complex societal prejudices we encounter today. This understanding is a key step in dismantling these outdated notions and building a more united and equitable world.

# Chapter 2: The Psychology Behind Prejudice

## Cognitive Biases and Stereotyping

### What Are Cognitive Biases?

Imagine your brain as a busy office worker, overloaded with information. To manage, it takes shortcuts, often leading to quick but inaccurate judgments. These shortcuts are called cognitive biases. They're like instinctive filters through which we see the world, often without even realizing it.

### Stereotyping: The Shortcut to Judgment

One common shortcut is stereotyping. This is when we assign traits to people based on the group they belong to, rather than their individual qualities. For instance, thinking that all elderly people are bad with technology is a stereotype. It's like assuming every book in a genre has the same plot without reading them.

### The Impact of Stereotypes

Stereotypes might seem harmless, but they can lead to unfair and harmful judgments. They can make us overlook a person's unique qualities and abilities, leading to prejudice.

## Social Identity Theory: Us vs. Them

### Our Groups Define Us

Humans are social creatures; we like to belong to groups, whether they're based on hobbies, nationality, or favorite sports teams. This is where Social Identity Theory comes in. It suggests our group memberships play a big part in how we see ourselves.

### The In-Group Bias

We naturally favor our own groups (in-groups), seeing them in a positive light, while we're more critical of other groups (out-groups). It's like rooting for your home team and seeing the rival team in a less favorable way.

### The Need for a Positive Self-Image

We often enhance our self-esteem by seeing our in-groups as superior. If you're a fan of a particular music genre, you might see it as more sophisticated than others. This isn't just about music taste; it reflects on how you see yourself - as someone with refined tastes.

## The Role of Fear and Ignorance

### Fear: The Root of Prejudice

Fear is a powerful emotion and can be a significant driver of prejudice. When we're afraid, we're more likely to hold onto negative stereotypes and biases. This fear can stem from a lack of understanding, unfamiliarity, or past negative experiences.

## Ignorance: The Lack of Knowledge

Ignorance, or a lack of knowledge, often goes hand in hand with fear. When we don't know much about a particular group, we might fill in the gaps with stereotypes. It's like being afraid of the dark; the unknown is often more frightening than the reality.

## Breaking Down Fear and Ignorance

To combat fear and ignorance, education and exposure are key. Learning about different cultures and meeting people from diverse backgrounds can help dispel myths and reduce unfounded fears.

The psychology behind prejudice is complex, involving cognitive biases, our social identities, and often, our fears and lack of understanding. By becoming aware of these factors, we can start to question our automatic thoughts and reactions. This chapter is not just about understanding prejudice in others; it's a call to examine our own minds, to recognize and challenge the biases within us, and to move towards a more inclusive and understanding world.

# Chapter 3: Discrimination Unraveled

## Forms of Discrimination: Overt and Covert

### Overt Discrimination: Clearly Visible

Overt discrimination is like a bold, unwelcome sign at a shop door. It's obvious and easily seen. This type of discrimination is direct and blatant. For example, a job advertisement that specifies a preference for candidates of a certain race or gender is overt discrimination. It's like being told directly, "You are not welcome here because of who you are."

### Covert Discrimination: Hidden and Subtle

Covert discrimination is more like a whisper than a shout. It's not as easily spotted. This form of discrimination is hidden, subtle, and often socially normalized. Imagine a manager who always overlooks a particular group of employees for promotions, not because of their performance, but because of unconscious biases. This is covert discrimination – it's happening, but it's not as easy to point out.

# The Impact of Institutionalized Discrimination

## The Role of Institutions

Institutionalized discrimination is when the systems and structures of a society discriminate, either overtly or covertly. It's not just about one person's actions; it's about how rules, laws, and social norms can create and maintain inequality. Think of it as a game where the rules unintentionally favor some players over others.

## Examples in Everyday Life

This can be seen in areas like housing, where certain groups might be subtly discouraged from living in particular neighborhoods, or in education, where resources might be unevenly distributed across schools in different areas.

## The Ripple Effect

The effects of institutionalized discrimination are profound. They can limit access to education, jobs, and healthcare for certain groups, creating cycles of disadvantage that can last for generations.

## The Bystander Effect and Social Conformity

## The Bystander Effect: When Silence Speaks

The bystander effect occurs when people don't intervene in a discriminatory situation because they think someone else will, or they don't want to stand out. Imagine seeing someone being treated unfairly and thinking, "Someone else will surely help." This is the bystander effect in action.

## Social Conformity: Following the Crowd

Social conformity is when people go along with what they think is the group norm. If a group tolerates discrimination, its members might unconsciously adopt this tolerance, even if they personally disagree. It's like laughing along with a joke you find offensive because everyone else is laughing.

## Breaking the Cycle

To counter these phenomena, it's important to be aware of them and to actively choose to speak up and act against discrimination. This could be as simple as questioning discriminatory comments or practices, or supporting those who are being treated unfairly.

Discrimination, whether overt or covert, and whether at an individual or institutional level, has profound impacts on society. By understanding these forms of discrimination and the psychological phenomena like the bystander effect and social conformity, we can begin to take steps to challenge and change these patterns. This chapter isn't just about recognizing discrimination; it's about empowering each of us to be part of the solution in creating a fairer, more inclusive world.

# Chapter 4: Cultural Influences and Prejudice

## The Role of Media and Cultural Narratives

### Media: The Storyteller of Society

Think of media — television, movies, news, social media — as a powerful storyteller that shapes our understanding of the world and the people in it. Just like a gripping book, the stories media tells can deeply influence how we think and feel about others.

### Stereotypes in Media

Media often falls into the trap of stereotyping: portraying certain groups of people in oversimplified or exaggerated ways. For instance, a TV show might always show a particular ethnicity in negative roles or as the butt of jokes. These portrayals can reinforce existing prejudices, subtly suggesting that these stereotypes are true.

### Cultural Narratives: The Stories We Grow Up With

Cultural narratives are the stories and ideas that our culture hands down to us. They're like the background music of our lives, so constant that we sometimes don't notice them. These narratives include beliefs about gender roles, race, and social status, and they shape our perceptions from a young age.

## The Power of Representation

Positive representation in media can combat prejudice. When media showcases diverse and realistic portrayals of different groups, it can break down stereotypes. It's like opening a window in a room that's been closed off, letting in fresh air and new perspectives.

## Cross-Cultural Studies of Prejudice

### Learning from Different Societies

Cross-cultural studies look at how different societies and cultures view and handle prejudice. Imagine it as a world tour, where each stop offers a unique perspective on how people see and treat each other.

### Similarities Across Cultures

Despite cultural differences, some forms of prejudice are sadly universal. For instance, almost every culture has some form of in-group bias, favoring people who are seen as similar to themselves.

### Differences: Cultural Contexts

However, the way prejudice manifests can vary greatly between cultures. In some societies, class or caste might be the primary basis of prejudice, while in others, it might be race or ethnicity. These differences show how cultural context shapes the nature of prejudice.

**Learning and Adapting**

Studying these differences helps us understand the roots of prejudice and how cultural factors influence attitudes. It's like comparing notes with someone from a different background - you learn new ways of seeing and understanding the world.

In this chapter, we've explored how media and cultural narratives shape our perceptions and contribute to prejudice. We've also seen how looking at prejudice through a cross-cultural lens can provide valuable insights. Understanding these influences is key to recognizing and challenging our own biases. It's not just about changing the channel or rejecting harmful narratives; it's about actively seeking diverse perspectives and stories that broaden our understanding and empathy for others.

# Chapter 5: The Development of Prejudice in Individuals

**Childhood and the Formation of Prejudices**

**The Early Years: A Foundation for Attitudes**

Imagine a young child as a sponge, soaking up everything around them. This is how children form their understanding of the world. In these early years, their minds are incredibly open and malleable, meaning they easily absorb the attitudes, beliefs, and biases of those around them.

**Learning by Observing**

Children learn a lot by simply watching and imitating others, especially their parents and close family members. If a child sees a parent consistently reacting negatively to a particular group of people, the child may start to mimic these attitudes. It's like learning a dance by following someone else's steps.

**The Role of Play and Socialization**

Play is a crucial part of how children learn about social norms. Through play, they experiment with different roles and scenarios, which can sometimes include mimicking societal prejudices they observe. This can also be a stage where they start to learn about inclusion and empathy, depending on their interactions and guidance.

## The Role of Family, Peers, and Education

### Family: The First School of Thought

The family environment is often where the seeds of prejudice are first planted or prevented. Family conversations, attitudes, and even jokes can subtly influence a child's perceptions of different social groups. Positive family discussions about diversity and respect can be powerful in shaping open-minded attitudes.

### Peers: The Social Mirror

As children grow, their peer groups become increasingly influential. These are the friends they play with, the classmates they sit with at lunch, and the teammates in sports. Peers can reinforce or challenge prejudices. If a child is part of a group that values diversity and inclusiveness, they are more likely to adopt these values themselves.

### The Impact of Bullying and Exclusion

Negative peer interactions, like bullying or exclusion, can also shape prejudices. For example, if a child is bullied by someone from a different background, they may develop negative associations with that entire group.

### Education: Broadening Horizons

Schools play a critical role in either challenging or reinforcing prejudices. An inclusive curriculum that celebrates diversity and teaches about different cultures can broaden students' horizons. Conversely, a curriculum that overlooks certain groups or presents biased histories can perpetuate stereotypes.

## The Power of Critical Thinking

Education that encourages critical thinking helps students question stereotypes and form their own, more informed opinions. It's like teaching someone how to fish rather than just giving them a fish. They learn to analyze and understand the world more deeply.

The development of prejudice in individuals is a complex process influenced by various factors from childhood. Family, peers, and education are key players in this process. By understanding these influences, we can begin to see how prejudices are formed and, more importantly, how they can be prevented and dismantled. This chapter highlights the importance of proactive and positive influences in the early stages of life, setting the foundation for a more inclusive and empathetic mindset.

# Chapter 6: Psychological Theories and Prejudice

**Freudian Perspectives**

**The Mind's Inner Conflict**

Sigmund Freud, a famous psychologist, saw the human mind as a place of deep conflict and tension. According to Freud, our behavior is influenced by unconscious desires and fears. When it comes to prejudice, Freudian theory suggests that it may stem from unresolved internal conflicts or anxieties.

**Projection: Blaming Others for Our Fears**

A key Freudian concept is projection. This is when we take our own unwanted feelings and project them onto others. For example, if someone is uncomfortable with their own feelings of aggression, they might see others as threatening or aggressive. Prejudice, in this view, is like a mirror reflecting our own fears and insecurities onto others.

**Learning Theories: Conditioning and Social Learning**

## Conditioning: Learning Through Association

Conditioning is a process where we learn to associate certain things with certain responses. Classic conditioning can lead to prejudice if we consistently see negative portrayals of a group paired with negative ideas or emotions. It's like hearing ominous music every time a particular character appears in a movie, leading you to feel uneasy about them.

## Social Learning: Copying Behavior

Social learning theory, proposed by Albert Bandura, emphasizes the role of observation in learning. We often learn attitudes and behaviors by observing others, especially those we see as role models. If a child sees their parents or influential figures expressing prejudiced views, they may mimic these attitudes.

## Cognitive Dissonance and Prejudice

## The Clash of Conflicting Beliefs

Cognitive dissonance occurs when our beliefs are in conflict with our actions or other beliefs. It's like having two opposing thoughts in your mind at the same time, which can be uncomfortable. For instance, if someone believes in equality but also holds prejudiced views, this conflict can create internal discomfort.

## Justifying Prejudice

To reduce this discomfort, people might change their beliefs or justify their prejudice. They might seek out information that supports their prejudiced views, ignoring anything that contradicts them. It's like adjusting a picture frame to make sure it hangs the way you want, even if it's not straight.

In this chapter, we explored various psychological theories to understand prejudice. Freudian perspectives show us how our unconscious mind and internal conflicts might contribute to prejudicial attitudes. Learning theories, including conditioning and social learning, highlight how our environment and role models shape our beliefs. Finally, cognitive dissonance reveals the mental gymnastics we might perform to maintain prejudiced views despite conflicting beliefs. Understanding these theories helps us see prejudice not just as a societal issue but as a deeply personal one, woven into the fabric of our psychological makeup. This knowledge empowers us to confront and challenge prejudice both within ourselves and in the world around us.

# Chapter 7: The Impact on Victims

**Psychological Effects of Experiencing Discrimination**

**The Weight of Discrimination**

Experiencing discrimination is like carrying an invisible, heavy backpack every day. It's a burden that can have profound psychological effects on individuals. These effects can be immediate and also long-lasting, impacting a person's mental and emotional well-being.

**Emotional Turmoil**

Victims of discrimination often experience a range of intense emotions. This can include feelings of sadness, anger, helplessness, and fear. It's similar to feeling constantly undervalued or attacked for who you are, something deeply personal and integral to your identity.

**Self-Esteem and Identity**

Discrimination can severely impact a person's self-esteem and sense of identity. Constant negative treatment based on personal characteristics can lead to a diminished sense of self-worth. It's like being told repeatedly that your voice doesn't matter, which can make you question your own value.

## Mental Health Consequences

Long-term exposure to discrimination can lead to serious mental health issues like depression, anxiety, and stress-related disorders. It's akin to a constant state of stress or being on edge, never knowing when the next negative encounter will happen.

## Coping Mechanisms and Resilience

## Developing Coping Strategies

People who experience discrimination often develop coping mechanisms to deal with its effects. These strategies can be adaptive, like seeking support from loved ones or engaging in activism, or maladaptive, such as withdrawing from social interactions or internalizing negative beliefs.

## The Power of Support Systems

Having a strong support system, including family, friends, and community, is crucial. It's like having a safety net or a team of cheerleaders who provide emotional support, validation, and a sense of belonging.

## Resilience: Rising Above Challenges

Resilience is the ability to bounce back from negative experiences. It's like a muscle that gets stronger with use. Some people find strength in their cultural heritage, others in a sense of shared struggle and solidarity. Resilience doesn't mean the pain of discrimination goes away, but it provides a way to navigate and rise above it.

## Seeking Professional Help

Professional help, such as counseling or therapy, can be beneficial. Therapists can provide a safe space to process feelings, develop coping skills, and strengthen resilience. It's like having a guide in a difficult journey, offering support and direction.

The impact of discrimination on victims is profound and multifaceted. It affects their emotions, self-esteem, mental health, and overall well-being. However, through coping mechanisms and resilience, many find ways to endure and overcome these challenges. This chapter highlights the importance of understanding these impacts, not just for those who experience discrimination but for society as a whole. By recognizing the weight of this burden, we can better support those affected and work towards a more inclusive and empathetic world.

# Chapter 8: Countering Prejudice and Discrimination

## Role of Education and Awareness

### Planting Seeds of Understanding

Education is like a gardener planting seeds that can grow into understanding and acceptance. By educating people from a young age about different cultures, histories, and perspectives, we can counteract prejudice and discrimination. This kind of education is not just about facts; it's about fostering empathy and critical thinking.

### Breaking Down Stereotypes

Incorporating diverse perspectives in educational content helps break down stereotypes. It's like showing someone the full picture when they've only seen a part of it. Through books, discussions, and media that showcase the vast range of human experiences, we can challenge oversimplified and prejudiced views.

### Awareness Programs

Awareness programs in schools, workplaces, and communities play a crucial role. These programs can take many forms, like workshops, seminars, or cultural events, and aim to highlight the issues of prejudice and discrimination, promoting a culture of inclusivity.

## Psychological Interventions

### Individual Counseling

Counseling and therapy can help individuals unlearn prejudiced beliefs and develop healthier attitudes. This process is akin to unraveling a tightly wound ball of yarn — it takes time and effort but can lead to profound changes in how individuals perceive and relate to others.

### Group Therapy and Workshops

Group settings can be effective for discussing and addressing prejudices. In these safe spaces, participants can share experiences, confront their biases, and learn from each other. It's like a support group where everyone is working towards the common goal of understanding and respect.

### Cognitive-Behavioral Approaches

Cognitive-behavioral therapy (CBT) techniques can be used to challenge and change prejudiced thoughts. This approach involves identifying and questioning negative beliefs and replacing them with more positive and realistic ones.

## Legal and Policy Measures

### Anti-Discrimination Laws

Laws play a crucial role in combating discrimination. These laws are like the rules of a game, setting standards for how people should be treated regardless of their race, gender, religion, or other characteristics. They provide protection and avenues for redress for victims of discrimination.

## Workplace Policies

In the workplace, policies and practices that promote diversity and equality are essential. This includes fair hiring practices, diversity training, and clear procedures for addressing discrimination. It's like setting a code of conduct that ensures everyone is treated fairly.

## Policy Advocacy

Advocacy for policy change is another key element. This involves pushing for laws and policies that address systemic discrimination and promote equality. Advocates work like voices amplifying the need for change, influencing decision-makers, and shaping public opinion.

Countering prejudice and discrimination is a multifaceted task that requires efforts at both individual and societal levels. Through education, psychological interventions, and legal and policy measures, we can work towards a world where everyone is valued and treated fairly. This chapter is not just a guide but a call to action, urging each of us to play our part in creating a more just and inclusive society.

# Chapter 9: Case Studies

## Historical and Modern Instances of Prejudice and Discrimination

### Learning from the Past

Looking at historical instances of prejudice and discrimination is like opening a book of our collective history. These examples show us how deep-rooted these issues can be and how they have shaped societies.

### The Jim Crow Era in the United States

Consider the Jim Crow laws in the United States, a classic example of institutionalized racial discrimination. These laws, enforced until the mid-20th century, mandated segregation between white and African American people in public places. They were like unfair rules in a game, designed to disadvantage a particular group.

### Apartheid in South Africa

Apartheid in South Africa was another blatant form of racial segregation and discrimination, enforced by law. It created a divide in society, where people were treated vastly differently based on their race, affecting everything from education to personal relationships.

**Modern Instances**

In modern times, prejudice and discrimination have not disappeared; they have just taken new forms. For example, the rise of social media has led to new platforms for both spreading and combating hate speech.

**Workplace Discrimination**

Consider a more subtle form of discrimination, such as unequal pay or opportunities in the workplace. This might not be as obvious as Jim Crow or apartheid laws, but it still significantly impacts people's lives.

**Analysis of Successes and Failures in Combating Prejudice**

**Successes: Steps Towards Equality**

**The Civil Rights Movement**

The Civil Rights Movement in the United States is a powerful example of successfully combating prejudice. Through nonviolent protest and persistent activism, civil rights advocates brought significant changes, like the end of Jim Crow laws and the passing of the Civil Rights Act of 1964.

**Marriage Equality**

The movement for marriage equality is a more recent success story. It shows how sustained advocacy, legal battles, and changing public opinion can lead to significant societal shifts, in this case, legal recognition of same-sex marriage.

## Failures: Lessons to Learn

## Continued Racial Disparities

Despite the successes of the Civil Rights Movement, racial disparities in areas like wealth, health, and criminal justice persist. These ongoing issues highlight the complexity of fully eradicating systemic prejudice.

## Refugee and Immigrant Discrimination

The ongoing discrimination against refugees and immigrants in many countries shows how fear and misunderstanding can lead to widespread prejudice. Despite international laws and human rights conventions, many refugees and immigrants still face hostile environments.

Studying both historical and modern instances of prejudice and discrimination, along with the successes and failures in addressing them, offers valuable lessons. It shows us that while progress has been made, the fight against prejudice is ongoing. Each case study serves as a reminder of the work that still needs to be done and the importance of continued vigilance and action against discrimination in all its forms. This chapter is not just a look back at history; it's a roadmap for the future, guiding us towards a more equitable and just society.

# Chapter 10: Future Directions

## Emerging Research and Theories

## Navigating New Frontiers in Understanding

In the realm of prejudice and discrimination, ongoing research continues to unveil new insights. Emerging research is like a ship exploring uncharted waters, seeking to understand the depths of these complex issues better.

### The Neuroscience of Prejudice

Modern neuroscience is shedding light on how prejudice works in the brain. Researchers are using brain imaging to study how we process information about 'others' and how biases are formed and maintained. It's like using a high-powered microscope to see the inner workings of the mind.

### Intersectionality

Intersectionality is a concept that looks at how different aspects of a person's identity (like race, gender, class) intersect and contribute to unique experiences of discrimination. It's like examining a multifaceted gem, where each facet represents a different part of a person's identity.

## The Role of Technology and Globalization

### Technology: A Double-Edged Sword

Technology, especially the internet and social media, has drastically changed how we communicate and interact. It can be a tool for spreading awareness and fostering understanding, but it can also be used to spread hate and misinformation.

### Social Media and Awareness

Platforms like Twitter, Facebook, and Instagram have given people a space to share their experiences with prejudice and discrimination, raising awareness on a global scale. Campaigns and movements often gain traction through these platforms, highlighting issues that may have otherwise gone unnoticed.

### Cyberbullying and Online Hate Speech

However, the anonymity and reach of the internet also make it easier for people to engage in cyberbullying and spread hate speech. Tackling these issues requires new strategies and approaches, considering the global and borderless nature of the internet.

### Globalization: Connecting and Clashing Cultures

Globalization has made the world more interconnected than ever. People from vastly different cultures are interacting more frequently, both in person and online. This increased interaction can lead to greater understanding and tolerance but can also result in clashes and an increase in prejudice.

## The Global Exchange of Ideas

The free flow of information across borders allows for an unprecedented exchange of ideas and perspectives. This can lead to a broader understanding and appreciation of different cultures.

## The Challenge of Cultural Sensitivity

On the flip side, this exchange can sometimes lead to cultural misunderstandings and the perpetuation of stereotypes. It highlights the need for cultural sensitivity and the importance of understanding the context behind cultural practices and beliefs.

Looking towards the future, the fight against prejudice and discrimination continues to evolve. Emerging research and theories provide new insights, while technology and globalization present both challenges and opportunities. This chapter points to a future where understanding, tolerance, and respect are more attainable, but also a future that requires vigilance, adaptability, and a commitment to embracing our increasingly interconnected world.

# Conclusion: Towards a More Inclusive World

## Reflecting on the Journey of Understanding

### The Path Traveled

As we conclude this exploration into the realms of prejudice and discrimination, it's like reaching the end of a challenging but enlightening hike. We've traversed through the historical landscapes, delved into the psychological underpinnings, witnessed the impacts on individuals, and glimpsed the potential paths ahead. This journey has not just been about acquiring knowledge; it's about reshaping our understanding and perspective.

### Lessons Learned

From the early roots of in-group vs. out-group dynamics to the modern complexities of discrimination in a digital age, we've seen how deep and multifaceted these issues are. We've learned that prejudice isn't just a social or historical problem; it's a personal one that exists in the biases and assumptions that each of us carries.

# The Role of Each Individual in Combating Prejudice and Discrimination

## The Power of the Individual

Every journey begins with a single step, and the journey towards a more inclusive world is no different. The role of the individual in combating prejudice and discrimination is paramount. It's about recognizing that each of us holds the power to effect change, whether in small daily interactions or in larger societal contexts.

## Self-Reflection and Awareness

The first step is self-reflection. It's about examining our own beliefs and attitudes, questioning where they come from, and being honest about our biases. This internal work is like tending to our own garden, ensuring that the seeds of prejudice don't take root.

## Speaking Out and Taking Action

Beyond self-reflection, it's about speaking out and taking action. This can be as simple as challenging a prejudiced remark in a conversation, or as involved as participating in community efforts to promote inclusivity. Every action, no matter how small, contributes to the larger movement towards change.

## Education and Continuous Learning

Continuous learning and education are also key. Staying informed, listening to diverse perspectives, and educating others plays a vital role. It's like keeping the map updated in a rapidly changing world.

## Building Empathy and Understanding

Building empathy and understanding is crucial. This means stepping into others' shoes, appreciating their experiences, and recognizing our shared humanity. It's about moving beyond tolerance to genuine acceptance and appreciation of diversity.

As we wrap up this journey, it's clear that the road to a more inclusive world is ongoing and requires the collective effort of all individuals. The fight against prejudice and discrimination is not just about policies and laws; it's about the choices we make every day, the conversations we have, and the way we see and treat each other. This chapter, and indeed this entire exploration, is an invitation to each of us to play our part in creating a world where diversity is celebrated, and every individual is valued and respected.

# About Freudian Trips

Welcome to Freudian Trips, your dedicated platform for diving deep into the world of psychology. We are more than just a YouTube channel or a book publisher. We are a beacon of enlightenment, making complex psychological concepts accessible and engaging for all.

Our YouTube channel is a rich repository of psychology made simple. We take the profound and often complex ideas from the world of psychology and break them down into digestible, easy-to-understand content. From the foundational theories of Freud to the cognitive insights of Piaget, we cover a broad spectrum of psychological schools and thoughts, making psychology accessible to everyone, regardless of their background or prior knowledge.

As a book publisher, we take the same approach, transforming intricate psychological theories into comprehensible narratives. Our books are not just collections of words, but vessels of wisdom that make psychology approachable and relatable. We believe that psychology should not be confined to academic circles, but should be available to all who seek to understand the human mind and behavior.

At Freudian Trips, we believe in the power of curiosity and the pursuit of knowledge. We are here to stoke the fires of your curiosity, to guide you on your intellectual journey, and to help you navigate the fascinating world of psychology.

If you are someone who is not afraid to question, to explore, and to learn, then you are in the right place. Join us on this journey of exploration, as we make psychology easy to understand, one concept at a time.

Be sure to visit our Youtube channel at: www.freudiantrips.com/youtube

You can also visit us on the web at www.freudiantrips.com

Welcome to The Freudian Trip community. Stay curious. Stay enlightened.